Revelation: Background and Commentary

Robert C. Jones

jone442@bellsouth.net
www.sundayschoolcourses.com

First Edition

ISBN: 1456595997
EAN-13: 978-1456595999

Table of Contents

Introduction

In the many years that I've been teaching adult Sunday School and leading Bible studies, Revelation remains the single most requested book of the Bible. Yet Revelation is also one of the most difficult books in the Bible to interpret – and, indeed, a wide range of interpretations have been offered up over the 1,900 years since it was written.

How one interprets Revelation often reflects on one's personal theological and even political views. Interpretations range from "it's all metaphor" to "it's a blueprint for the future". Major theories would include:

1. The prophecies and events described are concerned only with events in John's day, and have no bearing on today or the future. In this view, Revelation is more about 1st century Roman persecution of Christians (Nero, etc.) than it is about anything else.
2. Revelation is a description (and preview) of history from John's time to the end of the world. In this view, it is possible to identify in Revelation major historical events that have already occurred.
3. Revelation is a description of events that will occur in the "end times", or at the end of the world. Thus, none of the events after Chapter Three have yet occurred. This was the view of many in early church, and also of many modern day Evangelicals.
4. Revelation is a metaphor for the ultimate triumph of God over evil. Thus, one shouldn't expect to find actual events (past, present or future) in Revelation.

In the name of full disclosure, my view is #3 above, and the chapter-by-chapter commentary will reflect that view.

In this study, we'll begin by positioning Revelation among the long Jewish and early Christian tradition of apocalyptic writings – including the period "between the Testaments". We'll finish with a chapter-by-chapter look at Revelation itself.

Cathedral of the Plains , Victoria, Kansas (Photo by Robert C. Jones)

Nomenclature, author and date

Revelation is referred to by various different names in different Bibles and translations, perhaps reflecting the general unease that has accompanied study of this book for the last 1,900 years. Among the titles one will find:

- Revelation (the Latin form of *apocalypse*)
- Revelation of John
- Revelation of St. John the Divine ("Divine" in this case meaning "theologian", from the Greek *theologos*)
- Revelation of Jesus Christ to St. John
- The Apocalypse (which comes from the Greek *apokalypsis*, meaning "to uncover, to reveal")

In common parlance, "apocalypse" is sometimes also used to refer to the Second Coming of Jesus Christ.

The traditional author of Revelation is John the Apostle. However, in recent years, some scholars have questioned apostolic authorship. (The author refers to himself simply as "John" (Rev. 1:1, 1:4, 1:9, 22:8)). As backing for a non-apostolic authorship, some scholars point to the fact that Revelation is written in a crude Greek style significantly different than the Gospel of John. (One counter-theory is that Revelation was originally written in Aramaic, and (crudely) translated into the Greek version we have today.)

The John the Apostle connection comes from this passage in the first Chapter of Revelation:

> I, John, your brother and companion in the suffering and kingdom and patient endurance that are ours in Jesus, was on the island of Patmos because of the word of God and the testimony of Jesus. (NIV, Rev. 1:9)

John on Patmos, Cathedral of the Plains , Victoria, Kansas (Photo by Robert C. Jones)

There is a great body of early church tradition that identifies the author as being John the Apostle (see section "The authority of Revelation"), and also associating John the Apostle with an exile on Patmos.

According to Hippolytus (170-236 A.D.), John was banished by Domitian to the Isle of Patmos, and later died in Ephesus (one of the 7 churches referenced in Revelation):

> John, again, in Asia, was banished by Domitian the king to the isle of Patmos, in which also he wrote his Gospel and saw the apocalyptic vision; and in Trajan's time he fell asleep at Ephesus, where his remains were sought for, but could not be found. (*On*

the Twelve Apostles, Hippolytus, Translated by A. Cleveland Coxe, D.D.[1])

Eusebius (c. 260-c. 340 A.D.; Bishop of Caesarea), author of *Church History* in 325 A.D., records:

> ...Asia to John, who, after he had lived some time there, died at Ephesus. (Eusebius, *Church History*, translated by Arthur Cushman McGiffert, Ph.D.[2])

> It is said that in this persecution [Domitian] the apostle and evangelist John, who was still alive, was condemned to dwell on the island of Patmos in consequence of his testimony to the divine word. (Eusebius, *Church History*, translated by Arthur Cushman McGiffert, Ph.D.[3])

Eusebius also records that John outlived Domitian:

> At that time the apostle and evangelist John, the one whom Jesus loved, was still living in Asia, and governing the churches of that region, having returned after the death of Domitian from his exile on the island... [Irenaeus] in the second book of his work Against Heresies, writes as follows: "And all the elders that associated with John the disciple of the Lord in Asia bear witness that John delivered it to them. For he remained among them until the time of Trajan." (Eusebius, *Church History*, translated by Arthur Cushman McGiffert, Ph.D.[4])

Given that the emperor Domitian began his rule in 81 A.D., and died in 96 A.D., is it possible that John the Apostle could have still been alive by 96 A.D.? If John was in his late teens at the time of the death of Jesus in c. 30 A.D, he would have been in his 80s or 90s when he died. Certainly a reasonable possibility

---

1   *The Ante-Nicene Fathers Volume 5*, Edited by A. Roberts and J Donaldson
2   *The Nicene and Post-Nicene Fathers Second Series, Volume 1*, by Philip Schaff, editor, Ages Software 1999
3   *Ibid*
4   *Ibid*

Eusebius also records the words of Clement of Alexandria regarding the preaching and establishment of churches in Asia by John the Apostle:

> For when, after the tyrant's death, he returned from the isle of Patmos to Ephesus, he went away upon their invitation to the neighboring territories of the Gentiles, to appoint bishops in some places, in other places to set in order whole churches, elsewhere to choose to the ministry some one of those that were pointed out by the Spirit... (Eusebius, *Church History*, translated by Arthur Cushman McGiffert, Ph.D.[5])

There is no compelling evidence to doubt that John the Apostle was the author of Revelation.

Most scholars put the date of the writing of Revelation at the end of the reign of Roman Emperor Domitian (95/96 A.D.) Early Church Father Iranaeus reported that it had been written during the reign of Domitian (81-96 A.D.). Some scholars think it could have been as early as Nero's reign (68 A.D.), based on a literal interpretation of Rev. 11:1-2 (Jerusalem was destroyed in 70 A.D.)

I'd prefer a date in the late 80s/early 90s, making it the last book of what later became the New Testament to be written.

---

5   *Ibid*

The authority of Revelation

The view that Revelation is sacred scripture dates back to the earliest days of the Church. For example, Irenaeus (Bishop of Lyons from 177-202 A.D.) in his extant works (primarily, "Against Heresies"), quoted from 22 books of the New testament – including Revelation.

Origen (185-253 A.D.) connected Revelation with John the Apostle:

> John, who has left us one Gospel...also the Apocalypse...He has left also an epistle of very few lines; perhaps also a second and third; but not all consider them genuine, and together they do not contain hundred lines. (Eusebius, *Church History*, translated by Arthur Cushman McGiffert, Ph.D.[6])

Early lists of potential New Testament books			
Irenaeus (c. 180)	Muratori Canon (c. 200)	Eusebius (c. 325)	Athanasius (367 A.D.)
Matthew	(Matthew)	Matthew	Matthew
Mark	(Mark)	Mark	Mark
Luke	Luke	Luke	Luke
John	John	John	John
Acts	Acts	Acts	Acts
Romans	Romans	Romans	Romans
I Cor.	I Cor.	I Cor.	I Cor.
II Cor.	II Cor.	II Cor.	II Cor.
Galatians	Galatians	Galatians	Galatians
Ephesians	Ephesians	Ephesians	Ephesians
Philippians	Philippians	Philippians	Philippians
Colossians	Colossians	Colossians	Colossians
I Thess.	I Thess.	I Thess.	I Thess.
II Thess.	II Thess.	II Thess.	II Thess.
I Timothy	I Timothy	I Timothy	I Timothy

6   *The Nicene and Post-Nicene Fathers Second Series, Volume 1*, by Philip Schaff, editor, Ages Software 1999

Early lists of potential New Testament books			
Irenaeus (c. 180)	Muratori Canon (c. 200)	Eusebius (c. 325)	Athanasius (367 A.D.)
II Timothy	II Timothy	II Timothy	II Timothy
Titus	Titus	Titus	Titus
			Philemon
			Hebrews
James [?]			James
I Peter		I Peter	I Peter
			II Peter
I John	I John	I John	I John
	II John		II John
			III John
	Jude		Jude
Revelation of John	Revelation of John	Revelation of John [?]	Revelation of John
Shepherd of Hermas	Wisdom of Solomon (Apocrypha)		
	Revelation of Peter		

The earliest known "canon" (list of books that would later make up the New Testament) also contained Revelation. The Muratori Canon is a fragmentary list (85 lines) dating to c. 200 A.D., named after its 18th century discoverer, Lodovico Muratori.

Church Historian Eusebius, writing in his *Church History* in c. 325, had a list of "accepted" and "rejected" books. Perhaps indicating that Revelation was controversial even in the 4th century, Eusebius placed it on...both lists!

Accepted

SINCE we are dealing with this subject it is proper to sum up the writings of the New Testament which have been already mentioned. First then must be put the holy quaternion of the

11

Gospels; following them the Acts of the Apostles. After this must be reckoned the epistles of Paul; next in order the extant former epistle of John, and likewise the epistle of Peter, must be maintained. After them is to be placed, if it really seem proper, the Apocalypse of John, concerning which we shall give the different opinions at the proper time. These then belong among the accepted writings. (Eusebius, *Church History*, translated by Arthur Cushman McGiffert, Ph.D.[7])

Disputed/Rejected

But of the writings of John, not only his Gospel, but also the former of his epistles, has been accepted without dispute both now and in ancient times. But the other two are disputed. In regard to the Apocalypse, the opinions of most men are still divided. But at the proper time this question likewise shall be decided from the testimony of the ancients. (Eusebius, *Church History*, translated by Arthur Cushman McGiffert, Ph.D.[8])

Among the disputed writings...as I said, the Apocalypse of John, if it seem proper, which some, as I said, reject, but which others class with the accepted books. (Eusebius, *Church History*, translated by Arthur Cushman McGiffert, Ph.D.[9])

In 367 A.D., Athanasius (c. 296-373 A.D.; Bishop of Alexandria) published his "the thirty-ninth Letter of Holy Athanasius, Bishop of Alexandria, on the Paschal festival". Contained in this letter was the complete list of books that make up our New Testament canon today. Revelation was on the list, where it has remained ever since.

Again it is not tedious to speak of the [books] of the New Testament. These are, the four Gospels, according to Matthew, Mark, Luke, and John. Afterwards, the Acts of the Apostles and Epistles (called Catholic), seven, viz. of James, one; of Peter, two;

---

7   *The Nicene and Post-Nicene Fathers Second Series, Volume 1*, by Philip Schaff, editor, Ages Software 1999
8   *Ibid*
9   *Ibid*

of John, three; after these, one of Jude. In addition, there are fourteen Epistles of Paul, written in this order. The first, to the Romans; then two to the Corinthians; after these, to the Galatians; next, to the Ephesians; then to the Philippians; then to the Colossians; after these, two to the Thessalonians, and that to the Hebrews; and again, two to Timothy; one to Titus; and lastly, that to Philemon. And besides, the Revelation of John. (Athanasius, *Festal Letter 39*[10])

---

10 *The Nicene and Post-Nicene Fathers Second Series, Volume 4*, by Philip Schaff, editor, Ages Software 1999

Apocalyptic literature

Revelation is written in the style of *apocalyptic* literature, which often includes elements such as:

- Use of vivid imagery and symbolism
- Often focused on eschatological (end times) issues
- Reference to a final reckoning between good and evil, with the people of God being rewarded, and the followers of Satan being punished
- A connection between the end times and the messiah
- Descriptions of heaven and hell
- Descriptions of a new heaven and a new Jerusalem
- Descriptions of Satan (Belial in the Dead Sea Scrolls) and his supporters
- Descriptions of a coming time of tribulation
- Raising of the dead

These descriptions are often communicated to the person having the vision by a dialogue with an angel or other heavenly being. The angel will often ask unanswerable questions, with the visionary replying "surely you know".

The style was not uncommon in Second Temple Judaism, and even before. Books such as Daniel, Ezekiel, Isaiah, Enoch, and 2nd Esdras all contain these elements, as do the Gospels, and the letters of Peter and Paul. The Dead Sea Scrolls also contain apocalyptic references (*War of the Sons of Light Against the Sons of Darkness*). In fact, one could make the statement that Revelation is a compendium of Second Temple and earlier apocalyptic works, adding a few unique elements.

Old Testament

The Old Testament contains much apocalyptic literature, although perhaps not in as concentrated a form as Revelation! Almost the whole second half of Daniel is apocalyptic, as are full chapters of Ezekiel and Zechariah. The table below gives some examples (it is not meant to be exhaustive).

Reference	Notes
Isaiah 6	A description of heaven (compare with Rev. 4/5)
Isaiah 24	A coming tribulation ("Therefore earth's inhabitants are burned up, and very few are left." (NIV, Is 24:6)
Isaiah 26:19	Raising of the dead
Isaiah 65:17-25	A new heaven and a new earth
Ezekiel 1	A vision of heaven; four living creatures; wheels within wheels
Ezekiel 37:1-14	Valley of Dry Bones – may be referring to a future raising of the Dead
Ezekiel 37, 38	Gog and Magog
Daniel 7	• Beasts and horns • The Ancient of Days on the throne • "…one like a son of man, coming with the clouds of heaven." (NIV, Dan 7:13)
Daniel 8	• Dialogue with Gabriel • "…a stern-faced king, a master of intrigue, will arise. He will become very strong, but not by his own power. He will cause astounding devastation and will succeed in whatever he does." (NIV, Dan 8:23/24) - a description of the antichrist?
Daniel 9:20-27	• Dialogue with Gabriel • Coming of the "Anointed One" • "The Abomination that Causes

Reference	Notes
	Desolation" – may be the antichrist, patterned after Antiochus Epiphanes IV
Daniel 11:29-36	The Abomination that Causes Desolation
Daniel 12	• A great tribulation; rise of Michael the archangel • Resurrection of the dead
Joel 2:28-32	Day of the Lord
Amos 5:18-20	Day of the Lord
Zechariah 1:7-17	Four horseman
Zechariah 4:1-14	Golden lampstands
Zechariah 6:1-8	Four horses
Zechariah 13:7-9	Coming tribulation
Zechariah 14:1-9	Day of the Lord
Malachi 4:1-3	Day of the Lord

New Testament

The New Testament, like the books of the prophets in the Old Testament, has many apocalyptic allusions outside of Revelation, including all four Gospels, and the letters of Peter, Paul, and Jude.

Reference	Notes
Matthew 13:37-43	End of the age; weeping and gnashing of teeth
Matthew 16:27	Second coming and final judgment
Matthew 24; Mark 13; Luke 21:5-36	The "mini-Apocalypse" • False prophets • Gospel preached throughout all the world • Abomination that causes desolation • Time of tribulation • Coming of the Son of Man • No one knows the hour
Matthew 26:64	Coming on the clouds of heaven
John 5:21-30	Raising of the dead; final judgment
John 12:31	"Now is the time for judgment on this

Reference	Notes
	world; now the prince of this world will be driven out." (NIV)
1 Corinthians 15:51-52	"Listen, I tell you a mystery: We will not all sleep, but we will all be changed—in a flash, in the twinkling of an eye, at the last trumpet. For the trumpet will sound, the dead will be raised imperishable, and we will be changed." (NIV)
1 Thessalonians 4:13-18	• Coming of the Lord • Raising of the dead • Vs. 17 is where the word "rapture" comes from – in Jerome's Vulgate, *rapiemur* means to "seize, snatch, carry away"
2 Thessalonians 1:5-10	"This will happen when the Lord Jesus is revealed from heaven in blazing fire with his powerful angels." (NIV, verse 7)
2 Thessalonians 2:1-12	Man of Lawlessness – probably the antichrist or the false prophet (Rev. 13)
2 Peter 3:3-13	Day of the Lord; Verses 10,12 sound to many people like nuclear war
Jude 1:14-15	"See, the Lord is coming with thousands upon thousands of his holy ones to judge everyone..." (NIV)

Apocrypha

In the Apocrypha (mostly made up of books that appear in a Second Temple Greek translation of the Hebrew scriptures), one can see an increasing emphasis on an afterlife, as well as on a final judgment against evil.

Wisdom of Solomon

The Wisdom of Solomon makes extensive references to an afterlife for the righteous, and a final punishment for the evil. Some examples:

[15]But the righteous live forever, and their reward is with the Lord; the Most High takes care of them.
[16]Therefore they will receive a glorious crown and a beautiful diadem from the hand of the Lord, because with his right hand he will cover them, and with his arm he will shield them.
(NRSV, Wisdom of Solomon, 5:15-16)

[20]They will come with dread when their sins are reckoned up, and their lawless deeds will convict them to their face.
[1]Then the righteous will stand with great confidence in the presence of those who have oppressed them and those who make light of their labors.
[2]When the unrighteous see them, they will be shaken with dreadful fear, and they will be amazed at the unexpected salvation of the righteous.
[3]They will speak to one another in repentance, and in anguish of spirit they will groan, and say,
[4]"These are persons whom we once held in derision and made a byword of reproach—fools that we were! We thought that their lives were madness and that their end was without honor".
(NRSV, Wisdom of Solomon, 4:20-5:4)

2 Maccabees

2 Maccabees has several passages that indicate a Jewish belief in the resurrection of the dead, and a final judgment day. One section discusses the martyrdom of seven brothers, who died rather than agree to eat pork. The brothers are defiant partially because they believe in resurrection of the dead:

[9]And when he was at his last breath, he said, "You accursed wretch, you dismiss us from this present life, but the King of the universe will raise us up to an everlasting renewal of life, because we have died for his laws." (NRSV, 2 Maccabees 7:9)

[14]When he was near death, he said, "One cannot but choose to die at the hands of mortals and to cherish the hope God gives of being raised again by him. But for you there will be no resurrection to life!" (NRSV, 2 Maccabees 7:14)

[23]Therefore the Creator of the world, who shaped the beginning of humankind and devised the origin of all things, will in his mercy give life and breath back to you again, since you now forget yourselves for the sake of his laws. (NRSV, 2 Maccabees 7:23)

2 Esdras

2 Esdras is by far the most apocalyptic book in the Apocrypha (note: 2 Esdras doesn't appear in modern Roman Catholic Bibles). As is the case with Daniel and Revelation, the vision described in 2 Esdras is in the form of a dialogue between an angel (Uriel) and the receiver of the vision (Ezra). Some examples of the apocalyptic themes in 2 Esdras follow.

An end times messiah

[26]For indeed the time will come, when the signs that I have foretold to you will come to pass, that the city that now is not seen shall appear, and the land that now is hidden shall be disclosed. [27]Everyone who has been delivered from the evils that I have foretold shall see my wonders. [28]For my son the Messiah shall be revealed with those who are with him, and those who remain shall rejoice four hundred years. [29]After those years my son the Messiah shall die, and all who draw human breath. [30]Then the world shall be turned back to primeval silence for seven days, as it was at the first beginnings, so that no one shall be left. [31]After seven days the world that is not yet awake shall be roused, and that which is corruptible shall perish. [32]The earth shall give up those who are asleep in it, and the dust those who rest there in silence; and the chambers shall give up the souls that have been committed to them. [33]The Most High shall be revealed on the seat of judgment, and compassion shall pass away, and patience shall be withdrawn. [34]Only judgment shall remain, truth shall stand, and faithfulness shall grow strong. [35]Recompense shall follow, and the reward shall be manifested; righteous deeds shall awake, and unrighteous deeds shall not sleep. *[36]*The pit of torment shall appear, and opposite it shall be the place of rest; and the furnace of hell shall be disclosed, and opposite it the paradise of delight. *[37]*Then the Most High will say to the nations that have been raised from the dead, "Look now, and understand whom you have

denied, whom you have not served, whose commandments you have despised. ³⁸Look on this side and on that; here are delight and rest, and there are fire and torments." Thus he will speak to them on the day of judgment—³⁹a day that has no sun or moon or stars, ⁴⁰or cloud or thunder or lightning, or wind or water or air, or darkness or evening or morning, ⁴¹or summer or spring or heat or winter or frost or cold, or hail or rain or dew, ⁴²or noon or night, or dawn or shining or brightness or light, but only the splendor of the glory of the Most High, by which all shall see what has been destined. ⁴³It will last as though for a week of years. ⁴⁴This is my judgment and its prescribed order; and to you alone I have shown these things". (NRSV, 2 Esdras 7:26-44)

³¹And as for the lion whom you saw rousing up out of the forest and roaring and speaking to the eagle and reproving him for his unrighteousness, and as for all his words that you have heard, ³²this is the Messiah whom the Most High has kept until the end of days, who will arise from the offspring of David, and will come and speak with them. He will denounce them for their ungodliness and for their wickedness, and will display before them their contemptuous dealings. ³³For first he will bring them alive before his judgment seat, and when he has reproved them, then he will destroy them. ³⁴But in mercy he will set free the remnant of my people, those who have been saved throughout my borders, and he will make them joyful until the end comes, the day of judgment, of which I spoke to you at the beginning. (NRSV, 2 Esdras 12:31-34)

Judgment Day

⁷⁰He answered me and said, 'When the Most High made the world and Adam and all who have come from him, he first prepared the judgment and the things that pertain to the judgment." (NRSV, 2 Esdras 7:70)

³⁵For after death the judgment will come, when we shall live again; and then the names of the righteous shall become manifest, and the deeds of the ungodly shall be disclosed. (NRSV, 2 Esdras 14:35)

Resurrection of the dead

[16]And I will raise up the dead from their places, and bring them out from their tombs, because I recognize my name in them. (NRSV, 2 Esdras 2:16)

[31]Remember your children that sleep, because I will bring them out of the hiding places of the earth, and will show mercy to them; for I am merciful, says the Lord Almighty. (NRSV, 2 Esdras 2:31)

A time of tribulation

[1]Now concerning the signs: lo, the days are coming when those who inhabit the earth shall be seized with great terror, and the way of truth shall be hidden, and the land shall be barren of faith. (NRSV, 2 Esdras 5:1)

[6]And one shall reign whom those who inhabit the earth do not expect, and the birds shall fly away together; [7]and the Dead Sea shall cast up fish; and one whom the many do not know shall make his voice heard by night, and all shall hear his voice. [8]There shall be chaos also in many places, fire shall often break out, the wild animals shall roam beyond their haunts, and menstruous women shall bring forth monsters. (NRSV, 2 Esdras 5:6-8)

Dead Sea Scrolls

The Dead Sea Scrolls reflect a highly developed sense of the battle between good and evil (personified as *Belial*). One can also find references to an apocalyptic messiah, and a final judgment day.

War Scroll

The War of the Sons of Light with the Sons of Darkness[11]

The War of the Sons of Light with the Sons of Darkness, often shortened to simply the *War Scroll*, describes a war between the forces of the "sons of light" and the sons of darkness (led by Belial or Satan). The scroll begins with:

> At the beginning of the undertaking of the sons of light, they shall start against the lot of the sons of darkness, the army of Belial... And the dominion of the Kittim shall come to an end, so that wickedness shall be laid low without any remnant; and there shall

---

11 Library of Congress http://www.loc.gov/pictures/item/mpc2010000277/PP/

be no survivor of the sons of darkness. (*The War of the Sons of Light with the Sons of Darkness*, Translated by Millar Burrows[12])

It may be inferred that the scroll is describing an apocalyptic, end-times battle, although this is not outlined explicitly in the text. The text is very specific about the order of battle, the requirements for the leaders, the numbers of the troops of the sons of light, etc. At one point, it describes that the sons of light will have 28,000 men of war and 6,000 charioteers whom "shall pursue to destroy the enemy in the war of God, to eternal destruction."

In favor of the text being an account of an apocalyptic battle is the role assigned to the Angel Michael:

Today is his appointed time to lay low and to make fall the prince of the dominion of wickedness; and he will send eternal help to the lot he has redeemed by the power of the angel he has made glorious for rule, Michael, in eternal light, to give light in joy to all Israel, peace and blessing to the lot of God, to exalt among the gods the rule of Michael and the dominion of Israel over all flesh. (*The War of the Sons of Light with the Sons of Darkness*, Translated by Millar Burrows[13])

This is, of course, at least somewhat similar in tone to passages in the 12th chapter of Revelation.

1 Enoch

1 Enoch has numerous passages that refer to a final judgment. Presiding over the final judgment – the "Son of man" or the "Elect One".

Behold he comes with ten thousands of his saints, to execute judgment upon them, and destroy the wicked, and reprove all of flesh for every thing which the sinful and ungodly have done, and

---

12 *The Dead Sea Scrolls* By Millar Burrows, The Viking Press, 1961
13 *The Dead Sea Scrolls* By Millar Burrows, The Viking Press, 1961

committed against him. (1 Enoch, 2 Chapter, translation by Richard Laurence, LL.D., 1821[14]; compare with Jude 14-15)

O ye kings, O ye mighty, who inhabit the world, you shall behold my Elect one, sitting upon the throne of my glory. And he shall judge Azazeel [Satan], all his associates, and all his hosts, in the name of the Lord of spirits. (1 Enoch 54:5, translation by Richard Laurence, LL.D., 1821[15])

But then the time shall come, then shall the power, the punishment, and the judgment take place, which the Lord of spirits has prepared for those who prostrate themselves to the judgment of righteousness, for those who abjure that judgment, and for those who take his name in vain. (1 Enoch 59:5, translation by Richard Laurence, LL.D., 1821[16])

Who [the Elect one] shall judge all the works of the holy, in heaven above, and in a balance shall he weigh their actions. And then He shall lift up his countenance to judge their secret ways in the word of the name of the Lord of spirits, and their progress in the path of the righteous judgment of the God most high. (1 Enoch 60:11, translation by Richard Laurence, LL.D., 1821[17])

He sat upon the throne of his glory; and the principal part of the judgment was assigned to him, the Son of man. (1 Enoch 68:39, translation by Richard Laurence, LL.D., 1821[18])

---

14 *The Book of Enoch – From the Ethiopic*, Reprinted by Hoffman Printing Co., 1996
15 *Ibid*
16 *Ibid*
17 *Ibid*
18 *Ibid*

Commentary on Revelation

As mentioned in the introduction, my view of Revelation is that it is "a description of events that will occur in the "end times", or at the end of the world." If one views that Revelation is about a sequence of events that will occur in the future, is it possible to put together a broad list of events that will occur? Revelation makes this challenging, as it doesn't always proceed in a linear time line from chapter to chapter. However, one can make a guess in broad terms as to the sequence of events:

- Opening of the scroll with 7 seals by the Lion of Judah (Chapter 5 onwards)
- God causes a time of tribulation on earth
- God sends two witnesses to prophesize to mankind
- Satan and his forces fight back
- Christ Returns, and defeats the earthly powers at the battle of Armageddon
- Satan is bound in the abyss for 1000 years
- Millennial Rule of Christ and the Martyrs
- Satan is released, and consigned to Hell
- Judgment Day
- The New Heaven, the New Earth, the New Jerusalem
- God Reigns Eternally!

Chapter 1

Revelation shows its distinctiveness in the very first verse - it is the only book in the Bible that claims to be a "Revelation of Jesus Christ". It is also the only book in the Bible that offers a blessing to those who read it (Rev. 1:3). Some other notes on Chapter 1:

- The author is mentioned by name (John) three times in this chapter; the link with Patmos occurs in verse 9

- John is instructed by Jesus to write what he sees and send it to 7 churches in Asia Minor. The messages are directed to the "angel" or "messenger" of the 7 churches.
- In verse 19, we're told that some of the events described take place in the future – "Write therefore the things which you have seen, and the things which are, and the things which shall take place after these things". (NIV)
- In various verses, we see the use of the number "seven" – seven spirits, seven stars, seven lampstands. The number seven is significant because it was considered a heavenly number. It (like many other numbers in Revelation) is not necessarily always meant to be taken literally.

Chapters 2-3

Seven angels with seven scrolls – a street scene in Melbourne, Australia
(Photo by Robert C. Jones)

The letters to the seven churches (all located in what is now western Turkey) are variously interpreted as to either apply specifically to situations in those churches at the time, and have no broader significance, or to be taken as having an enduring message for all churches. Certainly, some of the issues associated with the various churches (lack of spiritual passion, succumbing to pagan or Gnostic influences, etc.) can be seen in congregations in the 21st century!

Ephesus

Ruins at Ephesus[19]

Ephesus was the largest city in Asia at the time. It was the home of John himself (except during his exile to Patmos). Although it had a large Christian population (in a church founded by Paul), the city was also a center of emperor worship, which meant that there would have been pressures on Christians to accept more than one god.

19 Library of Congress http://www.loc.gov/pictures/item/mpc2010000564/PP/

The congregation is commended for not following false prophets (the Nicolaitans were a Gnostic sect), and enduring hardships in Christ's name. However, they are also condemned because "you have forsaken your first love", which perhaps means that they were lacking in spiritual passion or focus.

Smyrna

Smyrna (now Izmir, Turkey) was a prosperous city in Asia Minor with a large Jewish community that showed bitter enmity toward Christians.

No criticism is leveled toward this church, and they are commended for remaining steadfast in the face of poverty and other afflictions. However, they are warned of future suffering (compare with Philadelphia).

The "second death" may refer to a lifetime without God.

Pergamum

Pergamum was a city of great heathen influence ("where Satan has his throne"). The congregation was commended for their steadfastness, but condemned for having some who succumbed to pagan (Balaam) or Gnostic (Nicolaitan) influences.

Thyatira

Thyatira was the home of many trade guilds. Membership in those guilds often required participation in licentious activities. This created a compromising situation for Christians.

While the congregation is praised for their faith and perseverance, they are also condemned for some who succumb to pagan and/or Gnostic influences.

Sardis

Sardis was a wealthy city known for its profligacy. The congregation is condemned for not being as "alive" as in times past. The metaphor of the thief in the night is introduced.

Philadelphia

Philadelphia (City of Brotherly Love) was a small city beset by earthquakes. Like Smryna, the local Jewish community had strong enmity towards Christians.

No criticism is leveled toward this church! It appears that the congregation will be protected from the coming Tribulation (compare with Smyrna.)

Laodicea

Laodicea was a large commercial, banking, transportation, and administrative center. The congregation was severely reprimanded for being "neither hot or cold", or lacking spiritual passion. "So, because you are lukewarm—neither hot nor cold—I am about to spit you out of my mouth." (NIV, vs. 16) However, the congregation is still given a chance to repent.

Chapter 4

Chapter 4 is a description of heaven, similar to Isaiah 6 or Ezekiel 1. We are told right at the beginning that this is a description of the future - "I will show you what must take place after this." (NIV, Rev 4:1)

References are made to God on his throne, and other heavenly creatures, including the twenty-four elders (by church tradition, the 12 patriarchs and the 12 apostles), the "living creatures" (compare with Ezekiel 1), and a multitude of angels that worship Him.

God the Father and Christ the Son in Heaven (Illustration by Gustave Dore[20])

Chapter 5

Chapter 5 is the start of the sequence discussed at the beginning of this commentary – the opening of the sealed scroll by the Lamb. We are told that only the Lamb is worthy to open the scroll "because you were slain, and with your blood you purchased men for God from every tribe and language and people and nation." (NIV, Rev 5:9) Clearly, the Lamb is Jesus.

- The "Lion of the tribe of Judah" refers to Genesis 49:9

20 *Milton's Paradise Lost*, Published by Henry Altemus, Philadelphia, date unknown

- The "Root of David" reference refers to (among other places) the genealogies of Christ in Matthew and Luke, which show Jesus as a direct descendent of King David

Chapter 6

Once the seals on the scroll are opened, the time of Tribulation begins.   By tradition, the horses and riders unleashed by the opening of the first four seals are known as "The Four Horsemen of the Apocalypse". They bring war, plague, economic dislocation (the rider on the black horse causes a whole day's work to be required just to eat) and death.

"Four Horsemen of the Apocalypse"[21]

21 Library of Congress http://www.loc.gov/pictures/item/2002712720/

c. 1873 lithograph[22]

During this period of tribulation on earth, one of the enduring questions is, "do Christians have to suffer through the tribulation?", or, to put it another way, when are God's living servants taken up to him? Those that believe that living Christians are taken up by God before the Tribulation believe in *pretribulation*. Those that believe that Christians must live through the Tribulation believe in *posttribulation*. Finally, those that believe that living Christians are taken up by God in the middle of the Tribulation (typically, during the mysterious visit of the Two Witnesses) believe in *midtribulation*. As you read through Revelation, look for clues as to whether Christians seem to still be alive during the Tribulation – and whether they are new converts.

22 Library of Congress http://www.loc.gov/pictures/item/92519085/

With the opening of the fifth seal, we see the first reference to a group that is singled out for special mention several times in Revelation – the martyrs, or those that have died in God's name. Martyrdom for Christians was certainly a topic of great interest during John's time, as Christians were persecuted from the time of Nero onwards. (Nero lighted Rome by burning Christians on tar-soaked crosses in 64 A.D.)

With the opening of the sixth seal, God really has the attention of people on earth – even the rich and mighty cower in caves!

Chapter 7

One of the frustrating things about interpreting Revelation is that it doesn't always proceed in a linear timeline. Chapter 6 ends with the statement "For the great day of their wrath has come, and who can stand?" (NIV, Rev 6:17), but Chapter 7 seems to discuss issues other than this "day of wrath".

Chapter 7 discusses the putting of a seal on the forehead of God's servants (compare with the "mark of the Beast" in Chapter 13). Is this mark to protect them during the Tribulation, or simply to mark them for the future? And who are these mysterious 144,000? They are assigned to the Twelve Tribes of Israel (notice the absence of Dan). Is this referring to the number of Jews that will be saved? And is the number meant to be taken literally? 12 (patriarchs or tribes) times 12 (apostles) is 144, so perhaps the number is meant to be taken symbolically.

Next, John sees "a great multitude that no one could count, from every nation, tribe, people and language" (NIV, Rev 7:9). Obviously now, we aren't just talking about Jews. We are told that "these are they who have come out of the great tribulation; they have washed their robes and made them white in the blood of the Lamb". Are these to be equated with the martyrs from Chapter 6 (both are said to be wearing white robes), or is this different group to be saved?

One other note. The exchange in verses 13/14 between John and the angel is a standard device in apocalyptic literature, where an angel asks a human an unanswerable question, and the human responds "Sir, you know". The same device is seen in *2 Esdras*, the *Shepherd of Hermes*, and other books.

Chapter 8

"Then the angel took the censer, filled it with fire from the altar, and hurled it on the earth..." (Currier & Ives lithograph, 1875)[23]

In Chapter 8, we're back in the main sequence – the opening of the seventh (and final seal). The opening of this seal causes lots of action – spearheaded by 7 angels with trumpets. After describing a series of horrible events involving the first four angels with

23 Library of Congress http://www.loc.gov/pictures/item/90708634/

trumpets (fire, poison, blackening of the sky), the chapter ends with a warning that the plagues brought by the next three angels with trumpets will be even worse!

Chapter 9

One can certainly make a strong case that the "star that has fallen from the sky to the earth" is none other than Satan (compare to Rev 12:4, which is explicitly about Satan). The star falling to earth may be in reference to Satan's fall from heaven. The "star" is given the "key to the shaft of the abyss", and certainly, the association between Satan and the Abyss is quite explicit in Revelation 20:3.

c. 1887 lithograph[24]

The king of the Abyss in Revelation 9:11 would also seem to be Satan:

> They had as king over them the angel of the Abyss, whose name in Hebrew is Abaddon, and in Greek, Apollyon. (NIV, Rev 9:11; both words mean "destroyer")

If the "angel of the abyss" is Satan, and his forces are unleashed by the fifth angel sounding his trumpet, it is perhaps an example of

---

24 Library of Congress http://www.loc.gov/pictures/item/var1994000724/PP/

35

God having dominion over everything; he can even use Satan to his own ends. And the text is very clear that these demon locusts led by the angel of the abyss can attack "only those people who did not have the seal of God on their foreheads" (NIV, Rev 9:4) – in other words, nonbelievers. There is some irony in this because in Revelation 13, Satan marshals nonbelievers to make a last ditch stand against God.

Medieval engraving[25]

Chapter 9 continues with the sixth angel sounding the trumpet, and 200,000,000 mounted troops are unleashed to kill a third of mankind. The chapter ends with a key observation:

25 Library of Congress   http://www.loc.gov/pictures/item/2002712727/

The rest of mankind that were not killed by these plagues still did not repent of the work of their hands; they did not stop worshiping demons, and idols of gold, silver, bronze, stone and wood—idols that cannot see or hear or walk. Nor did they repent of their murders, their magic arts, their sexual immorality or their thefts. (NIV, Rev 9 20-21)

It appears that even during the tribulation, nonbelievers still have the opportunity to repent – but refuse to do so.

Chapter 10

Chapter 10 is a break in the action to prepare readers for what is still to come – the mighty seventh trumpeting angel:

But in the days when the seventh angel is about to sound his trumpet, the mystery of God will be accomplished, just as he announced to his servants the prophets. (NIV, Rev 10:7)

The text describing a scroll that is sweet in the mouth but sour in the stomach may be a metaphor in anticipation of the (temporary) rise of Satan as an earthly power in Chapter 13. On the surface, false prophets can sound mighty good, but in the end they lead to death.

We're also informed in verse 4 that John sees some things in his vision that he cannot write down.

Chapter 11

The first part of the action-packed Chapter 11 concerns two witnesses sent by God to prophesize to mankind (mankind is given continual opportunities to repent during the Tribulation). The two witnesses, by tradition, are either Elijah and Enoch (the two Old Testament figures that didn't die, but were taken up to heaven), or Elijah and Moses. The latter view comes from an interpretation of this passage:

> These men have power to shut up the sky so that it will not rain during the time they are prophesying; and they have power to turn the waters into blood and to strike the earth with every kind of plague as often as they want. (NIV, Rev 11:6)

In the Old Testament, Elijah is given the power to control the rain (see 1 Kings 17:1), and Moses turns water into blood and unleashes other plagues in his battle with Pharaoh.

The two witnesses are killed by the "beast that comes up from the Abyss" (Satan or one of his minions), and left to rot in the streets of Jerusalem while the inhabitants gloat over them. Finally, they are taken up to heaven in a cloud.

The second part of Chapter 11 concerns the seventh angel sounding his trumpet, and as a result, "the kingdom of the world has become the kingdom of our Lord and of his Christ" (NIV, verse 15). Certainly the moment is significant, because the Ark of the Covenant is seen within the Temple. Because of the reference to a standing temple in the first and last verses of this chapter, some people believe that means that the end times won't come until the temple is rebuilt in Jerusalem.

There is a theory that John actually tells the same story three times in Revelation, with varying levels of detail. In this theory, the end of Chapter 11 is one of those three similar endings (Rev 16:16-21 and Rev 19:11-21 being the other two).

Angels at St. Patrick's Cathedral in Melbourne, Australia (Photo by Robert C. Jones)

Chapter 12

Chapter 12 is another chapter that isn't necessarily meant to be taken in linear sequence. It describes a battle in heaven between the archangel Michael and Satan, and could refer to Satan's original fall from heaven (see also Ezekiel 28:12-19, Isaiah 14:12-20, etc.)

The reference to the woman who is about to give birth is sometimes interpreted as Mary, Mother of Jesus, and sometimes interpreted as a metaphor for Israel, or all of humankind (*adam*).

Satan, who is defeated in battle with Michael, may have taken a third of the angels with him in his fall to earth (verses 4,9).

Other items of interest:

* Revelation 12:9 explicitly connects Satan with that "ancient serpent called the devil". Genesis itself never explicitly states that the serpent in the Garden of Eden is Satan.

- Satan is overcome by "the blood of the Lamb", and by the testimony of the brothers that were accused by Satan (Satan in Hebrew can be translated as "accuser")
- Satan is filled with fury because of his fall from heaven (verse 12) - and he'll try to take it out on the offspring of the woman (verse 17)

"St. Michael fighting the dragon"[26]

Chapter 12 appears to be background material for the rise of Satan against God described in Chapter 13 (and prefigured in Chapter 11).

---

26 Library of Congress http://www.loc.gov/pictures/item/90707832/

Chapter 13

Chapter 13 of Revelation is one of the most terrifying chapters of the Bible. It describes a beast from the sea and a beast from the earth - human minions of Satan that carry out his wishes. It describes in detail the period when Satan fights back against God, and appears to be winning for a time (of course, the final defeat of Satan has been assured since before the creation of the universe).

The beast from the sea is, by tradition, the *antichrist* (the word itself is not used in Revelation, although John uses the word in his letters, and the concept is used in other books of the Bible - see the table below). The beast is a political leader and receives his power and authority from Satan (verse 2). Verse 8 tells us that all inhabitants of earth will worship the beast from the sea - except those belonging to the Lamb.

The word antichrist in the Bible	
Reference	Notes
1 John 2: 18-19	Apostate Christians
1 John 2: 22	Deniers of Christ's Divinity
1 John 4:2-3	Spirits that deny Christ's Divinity
2 John 7	Deceivers who deny Christ

The concept of antichrist in the Bible	
Reference	Notes
Dan 7:7, 19-27	"Fourth Kingdom on earth", war against the saints
Dan 8:23-25	Will destroy the holy people
Dan 11:31-32	Desecration of the temple
Dan 11:36-39	Sets himself above God
Dan 9:27, 11:31; Mat 24:15	Abomination that causes desolation
Rev 13:1-10	Beast from the sea; power invested by the dragon

The second beast, the beast from the earth, is the false prophet - a religious or "moral" leader that can perform miracles. He sets up an image of the first beast to be worshiped. And he requires that everyone have a mark (the mark of the beast) on their right hand or forehead in order to engage in commerce. Christians of course would refuse this mark – and not be able to earn a living.

The mark itself - 666 - has long fascinated readers. The text tells us only that it is man's number. Various theories as to the meaning include:

- Each digit one less than perfect (7)
- "Primal Chaos" in Hebrew (letters in Hebrew have numeric equivalents)
- "Nero Caesar" in poor Hebrew
- "The Latin Kingdom" in Greek
- It could be all!!!

References to the concept of the false prophet in the Bible	
Reference	Notes
1 John 2:18-19,22; 1 John 4:3, 2 John 7	Apostates, deniers of Christ's Divinity
2 Thes 2:1-12	Man of Lawlessness - "doomed to destruction"
Mat 24:23-26, Mark 13:21-23	Beware of false Messiahs and prophets
Rev 13:11-18	Beast of the earth, with a human number (666)

Chapter 14

The first 5 verses of Chapter 14 discuss 144,000 people with God's mark on them, standing on Mt. Zion with Jesus. The group isn't explicitly identified, but seem to be those that have led a particularly pure life ("those that did not defile themselves with women"). The reference to "they were purchased from among men and offered as firstfruits to God and the Lamb" could refer that these were martyrs ("offered" as firstfruits), or could mean that they had been dedicated to God from birth (something like the Jewish Nazirites). Some people take the number 144,000 literally, and go so far as to posit that this is the sum total of people that will be saved in the history of the world. However, the number is probably metaphorical (12 times 12 times 1000), and seems to refer to a specific group.

Verses 6-13 concern he actions of three angels used as messengers. The first angel "had the eternal gospel to proclaim to those who live on the earth—to every nation, tribe, language and people" (compare to Matthew 24:14). This is significant, because it answers one of the criticisms of Christianity from nonbelievers – what about all those poor people that have never heard about Jesus? Are they damned? It appears that everyone will hear the gospel preached before the final judgment. The second angel proclaims that "Babylon is fallen", with "Babylon in this context probably referring to Rome (more in Chapter 17/18). The third angel describes what will happen to those that have the mark of the beast on them – they "will be tormented with burning sulfur in the presence of the holy angels and of the Lamb" forever (more on the lake of burning sulfur in Chapter 20).

The last section of Chapter 14 – verses 14-20 – contain some of the most vivid imagery in Revelation. The first part discusses an angel with a sickle – known as "the grim reaper" in common parlance. This may or may not be a reference to Jesus. Verse 14 seems to refer to Jesus - "one 'like a son of man'" (compare with Daniel 7), but some object to this analysis because a second angel seems to issue orders to him in verse 15. Verses 18 and 19 contain imagery regarding grapes, and the "winepress of God's wrath". *The Battle Hymn of the Republic* makes references to these verses; *The Grapes of Wrath* took its name from this imagery.

"The Destroying angel!" (c.1870 lithograph)[27]

27 Library of Congress http://www.loc.gov/pictures/item/92521778/

Chapter 15

Chapter 15 prepares us for "seven angels with the seven last plagues", after which, "God's wrath is completed". We are introduced to a group of people who had been " victorious over the beast and his image and over the number of his name". We are reminded once again that the end is very near.

Chapter 16

Chapter 16 describes the activities of the seven angels with seven bowls of God's wrath. The plagues seem to get more and more serious – all living creatures in the sea killed, rivers turning into blood, etc. Verse 9 reminds us that even at this late date, men can still repent.

Verses 13/14 remind us that Satan has many demons working for him. In this case, they "go out to the kings of the whole world, to gather them for the battle on the great day of God Almighty." The final battle is upon us!

Verse 15 is of special interest. It almost seems as if it is misplaced, perhaps belonging in the last chapter of Revelation. Is it possibly a translator or copyist error from long ago?

And then, the final battle is prepared for:

> Then they gathered the kings together to the place that in Hebrew is called Armageddon. The seventh angel poured out his bowl into the air, and out of the temple came a loud voice from the throne, saying, "It is done!" (NIV, Rev 16:16-17)

Armageddon in Hebrew means simply "hill of Megiddo", which seems as likely a place for the final battle to occur as anywhere else (Syrian tanks crossed this area in the 1967 and Yom Kippur wars).

The hill...

and plains of Megiddo (Photos by Barbara Brim)

The two verses are frustrating, because we're told that the kings gathered at the hill of Megiddo, but the text doesn't tell us any details of the battle! It is possible that Rev 19:11-21 gives these details (as opposed to describing yet another battle). Either way, it appears that the result of this battle ("it is done") is a completion of God's preparatory work for the Second Coming of the messiah. However, we'll have to wait 2½ more chapters for a description of the great event itself!

Chapters 17/18

Chapters 17/18 describe in some detail that fate of "Babylon the Great, the Mother of Prostitutes and of the Abominations of the Earth". We can assume that this is in reference to Rome, as verse 9 (Chapter 17) refers to "seven hills on which the woman sits". It is not surprising that John would want to single out the destruction of those responsible for decades of persecution of Christians, from Nero's burning of Christians, to the slaughter of Christians in the Coliseum. John ends the two chapters by specifying "In her was found the blood of prophets and of the saints" – another seeming reference to the persecution of Christians by Rome.

While John used the metaphor of the Romans as the most evil thing he could think of – as we might use Osama Bin Laden or Adolph Hitler today – there is no reason to assume that these two chapters can't be viewed as broader metaphors for the final destruction of mankind's most evil manifestations.

Chapter 19

In Chapter 19, we are rewarded with a description of the Second Coming of Jesus Christ (perhaps also meant to be a description of the elusive battle of Armageddon referred to in Chapter 16). Verse 7 prepares us for the great event by saying, "the wedding of the Lamb has come, and his bride has made herself ready". The final joining of Christ to the Universal Church is about to begin.

Woodcut by Albrecht Dürer (c. 1510)[28]

In verses 11-21, the return of Christ is described. Some notes:

- His name is the "Word of God" – perhaps another sign that John the Apostle wrote Revelation, as the idea of Jesus being the "Word" (Greek *logos*) is first introduced in the Gospel of John 1:1
- He is followed by the armies of heaven; however, the sword in the mouth of the "King of Kings and Lord of Lords" is sufficient by itself to vanquish the armies of the beast and the false prophet

---

28 Library of Congress http://www.loc.gov/pictures/item/2004665189/

- The beast and the false prophet are captured, and "thrown alive into the fiery lake of burning sulfur" (we have to wait until the next chapter to find out Satan's fate!)

Chapter 20

Chapter 20 describes the aftermath of the events described in Chapter 19. Satan is locked in the Abyss (from whence he came?) for 1,000 years.

The millennial rule of Christ is described in verses 4-6, where those that "had not worshiped the beast or his image and had not received his mark on their foreheads or their hands...came to life and reigned with Christ a thousand years."

The 1,000-year rule of Christ is another area of differing interpretation. Those that believe that this 1,000 years occurs after the Tribulation and the Second Coming believe in *premillennialism*. Some believe that the reign of the Universal Church prior to the events depicted in Revelation is the millennium rule of Christ. This view is known as *postmillennialism*. And, of course, there is a camp that believes that verses 4-6 should be taken metaphorically, and don't pertain to any particular period of Christ's rule. This is sometimes referred to as *amilliennialism*.

Verses 7-10 describe the final doom of Satan, who is released after 1,000 years for one more battle – Gog and Magog (see Ezekiel 38,39). The devil is defeated in short order, and thrown into the lake of burning sulfur, joining the two beasts from Chapter 13.

Verses 11-15 describe the "Last Judgment", where the dead are judged "according to what they had done". There is some debate as to whether this final judgment involves believers. After all, the message of the New Testament is that if you have faith in Jesus Christ, you'll be saved – a final judgment seems somehow redundant (unless this is where works, rather than faith matter –

but then this could lead us into the concept of different levels of heaven – I'll stay out of that argument!)

Regardless, "if anyone's name was not found written in the book of life, he was thrown into the lake of fire", to join Satan, the antichrist, and the false prophet. These three, by the way, are sometimes referred to as the "false trinity".

c. 1889 lithograph[29]

Chapter 21

With non-believers consigned to the lake of burning sulfur, Revelation ends with a description of the "new heaven" and the "new earth" – a new life for believers after the Second Coming and Judgment Day (see also Isaiah 65:17-25).

> Then I saw a new heaven and a new earth, for the first heaven and the first earth had passed away, and there was no longer any sea. I saw the Holy City, the new Jerusalem, coming down out of heaven from God, prepared as a bride beautifully dressed for her husband. And I heard a loud voice from the throne saying, "Now

29 Library of Congress http://www.loc.gov/pictures/item/var1994000740/PP/

the dwelling of God is with men, and he will live with them. They will be his people, and God himself will be with them and be their God. He will wipe every tear from their eyes. There will be no more death or mourning or crying or pain, for the old order of things has passed away." (NIV, Rev 21:1-4)

Key to this new era is that "now the dwelling of God is with men, and he will live with them", returning to the state of the Garden of Eden prior to the Original Sin. This is stressed in verse 22, when John notes that there is no temple in the New Jerusalem:

> I did not see a temple in the city, because the Lord God Almighty and the Lamb are its temple. (NIV, Rev 21:22)

Chapter 22

And, finally, we come to the end of the last book of the Bible – completing the cycle begun in Genesis thousands of years before. In verse 8, John reminds us that he witnessed these things first hand - "I, John, am the one who heard and saw these things." But when John tries to worship the angel that had shown these things to him, the angel replied, "Do not do it! I am a fellow servant with you and with your brothers the prophets and of all who keep the words of this book. Worship God!" (NIV, Rev 22:9)

In this Chapter, John is once more in dialogue with Christ himself, who says:

> Behold, I am coming soon! My reward is with me, and I will give to everyone according to what he has done. I am the Alpha and the Omega, the First and the Last, the Beginning and the End. (NIV, Rev 22:12-13)

THE TREE OF LIFE.
On either side of the river was there the Tree of Life which bare
twelve manner of fruits - Revelation Chap XXII 2

"On each side of the river stood the tree of life, bearing twelve crops of fruit..." (Currier and Ives, c. 1872)[30]

And while Revelation began with a promise of a blessing, it ends with a warning:

> I warn everyone who hears the words of the prophecy of this book: If anyone adds anything to them, God will add to him the plagues described in this book. And if anyone takes words away from this book of prophecy, God will take away from him his share in the tree of life and in the holy city, which are described in this book. (NIV, Rev 22:18-19)

---

30 Library of Congress http://www.loc.gov/pictures/item/2002697362/

This passage is sometimes applied to the whole Bible (or, at least, the New Testament), but in reality it probably refers only to Revelation itself. At the time that Revelation was written, there was no New Testament (nor would there be an official New Testament funtil c. 367 A.D.)

Sources

Title	Author	Publisher	Date
Art Explosion 600,000		Nova Dev.	1999
Church History	Eusebius; trans. by Arthur Cushman McGiffert, Ph.D.	Ages Software	1997
Holy Bible - New International Version		Zondervan Publishing House	1973
Holy Bible – New Revised Standard Version		Zondervan Publishing House	1989, 1993
The Ante-Nicene Fathers - Volume 5	Edited by A. Roberts and J Donaldson	Ages Software	1997
The Book of Enoch – From the Ethiopic	Translation by Richard Laurence, LL.D.	Hoffman Printing Co.	1996
The Dead Sea Scrolls	Millar Burrows	The Viking Press	1961
The Nicene And Post-Nicene Fathers Second Series, Vol. 1, Vol. 4	Philip Schaff, editor	Ages Software	1996, 1997
Milton's Paradise Lost		Henry Altemus,	N/A

Links
Library of Congress http://www.loc.gov/pictures/item/mpc2010000564/PP/
Library of Congress http://www.loc.gov/pictures/item/2002712720/
Library of Congress http://www.loc.gov/pictures/item/92519085/
Library of Congress http://www.loc.gov/pictures/item/90708634/
Library of Congress http://www.loc.gov/pictures/item/var1994000724/PP/
Library of Congress http://www.loc.gov/pictures/item/2002712727/
Library of Congress http://www.loc.gov/pictures/item/90707832/
Library of Congress http://www.loc.gov/pictures/item/92521778/
Library of Congress http://www.loc.gov/pictures/item/2004665189/
Library of Congress http://www.loc.gov/pictures/item/var1994000740/PP/
Library of Congress http://www.loc.gov/pictures/item/2002697362/

About the Author

Robert C. Jones grew up in the Philadelphia, Pennsylvania area. In 1981, he moved to the Atlanta, Georgia area, where he received a B.S. in Computer Science at DeVry Institute of Technology. From 1984-2009, Robert worked for Hewlett-Packard as a computer consultant. He now works as an author, researcher and videographer.

Robert is President of the Kennesaw Historical Society, and Director of Programs and Education for the Kennesaw Museum Foundation. He has written several books on Civil War and railroad themes including *Retracing the Route of Sherman's Atlanta Campaign and March to the Sea*, *Images of America: Kennesaw*, and *The W&A, the General, and the Andrews Raid: A Brief History*.

Robert is an ordained elder in the Presbyterian Church. He has written and taught numerous adult Sunday School courses. He is the author of *A Brief History of Protestantism in the United States*, *A Brief History of the Sacraments: Baptism and Communion*, *Heaven and Hell: In the Bible, the Apocrypha and the Dead Sea Scrolls*, *The Crusades and the Inquisition: A Brief History*, *Monks and Monasteries: A Brief History*, *The 25 Most Influential People in the Post-Apostolic Christian Church*, *Revelation: Background and Commentary* and *Meet the Apostles: Biblical and Legendary Accounts*.

Robert has also written several books on ghost towns in the Southwest, including *Death Valley Ghost Towns – As They Appear Today* and *Ghost Towns of the Mojave National Preserve*. He's also written extensively on ghost towns in Nevada, Arizona and New Mexico.

In 2005, Robert co-authored a business-oriented book entitled *Working Virtually: The Challenges of Virtual Teams*.

His interests include the Civil War, Medieval Monasteries, American railroads, ghost towns, hiking in Death Valley and the Mojave, and Biblical Archaeology.

robertcjones@mindspring.com
http://www.sundayschoolcourses.com/

Made in the USA
Charleston, SC
27 April 2011